EXPLORING THE ISLANDS, HISTORY, AND MYTHOLOGY OF GREECE

EXPLORING THE ISLANDS, HISTORY, AND MYTHOLOGY OF GREECE

TRISTAN EVERGREEN

CONTENTS

CHAPTER 1

Introduction to Greece's Islands, History, and Myt

Visiting Greece is a bucket list-worthy trip. If one is so lucky to find oneself there in some season, there are many things worth experiencing and knowing about Greece. This essay provides some information sharing what one knows about their islands, history, and mythology. I have master's level academic knowledge and have lived and traveled within the country for about six months.

Known as the official Hellenic Republic, Greece is located in southeastern Europe and consists of nine major geographic regions, including over 2,000 islands. With a population of about 11 million, Greece has recorded history going back over 3,000 years. It has one of the longest and richest cultural heritages of all the European countries. Surprisingly, the present-day population has decreased by 10 percent due to financial problems and changing quality of life. Tourists or refugees who can prove they can support themselves may have better success at relocating to Greece. Regardless of the decreasing population, tourism to Greece remains a delight. There are over 2,000 Greek islands to visit and many things to do. Speleologists are going to love the islands where rich traditions of caving and adventurous exploits have been maintained. There are caves with music and slide projection tours, combined with beer and archaeology too. Tailor-made holidays to Greece offer you the flexibility to travel at your own pace through its extensive and convenient inter-island ferry service. Ferries are comfortable, fast, and efficient. Gourmet travelers and naturalists can take special and organized trips to these places, including explorations in Greece's northern complex of karstic caves in Chalkidiki.

Explorations in the large network of linked caves of Mt Chelmos are embraced by renowned scientific cavers and leaders from around the world. Greece is blessed (or burdened) with over 6,000 caves waiting to be explored. Whether they are sun-drenched, wind-swept, fertile, or barren, islands never fail to stir the Greek imagination. No wonder. Islands anciently had unimaginable prowess and supernatural inhabitants, and then grew to be the domain of the Gods themselves. Here are a few of the Greek islands and their remaining place-lore. History has created Greece, and Greece has created history. The ancient civilization put fact and fancy together. The tales they told about themselves and their world were both real and imagined. Heroic myth and battlefield accounts have survived from ancient times. A visitor to Greece will hear of the monumental contests, the major players, the bloody result, and their lingering significance.

CHAPTER 2

The Geography of Greece and Its Diverse Islands

Most readers have heard of Greece but do not know exactly what the place is like. So far as geography is concerned, Greece is in many ways sharply set off from what we in the United States, at least, are used to. Most of us think of a country as comprised mainly of land, with only moderate water areas. In Greece, on the other hand, the opposite is true. Roughly, 81% of the area is water and 19%, land. As a result, we have only to look at a map of the world to appreciate that Greece is made up of many islands. Although no one can say exactly how many there are, there are nearly two thousand islands. Of these, the government assigns names to only about one hundred, settling the others in various ways. In fact, primary or large islands number about ten and in this Apostolos the Less Island Bay Land of Greece. Apostolos is shown with an arrow to indicate its location in the Aegean Sea. Respect, we might say named and unnamed islands amount to about fifty-two main units. If we even visited all these, we would cover only a small part of Greece. However, this situation is not so bad as it looks. The islands and areas near Greece are not organized in some sort of geographical chaos. For example, the various groups of islands form a loose ring around the Greek mainland. Most of the larger units, at that, have a certain amount of orderly arrangement in individual island location. Greece itself is on an isthmus running generally northeast to southwest, providing the mainland. In a rough way, the country amounts to a rough square, with the large island of Crete being at the lower or south center. The trip starting from Italy would cover about two hundred fifty miles to the Greek islands and another one hundred fifty miles for trips among the islands.

CHAPTER 3

Ancient Greek History: From Mycenae to Classical A

The history of Greece is long and steeped in mythology. Its first inhabitants were the Titans, and its most recent were the Greeks. In the fourteenth and thirteenth centuries BCE, the Mycenaeans wielded the strongest influence in the area. They left behind grand ruins, tombs, and a script, Linear B. The period following the collapse of the Mycenaean society is popularly known as Greece's Dark Ages. It is this era that saw a decline in art and wealth, commerce, reading, and learning. Perhaps even more significantly, during this time the script was forgotten, thus there exists no written account of events for the next 450 years.

The next significant era in Greek history was the Classical period, which is comprised of the Archaic and Hellenistic periods. The period, lasting from 800-300 BCE, is characterized by the expansion of the Greek culture and rivalry between city-states. The Classical era is when the majority of Ancient Greece's greatest contributions to humankind were made: philosophy, art, literature, drama, architecture, mathematics, and the foundations of Western thought and civilization. This is often considered to be Athens' 'Golden Age'. At 508

BCE Athens established the world's earliest democratic government. In the battle of Marathon in 490 BCE, the Greeks defeated the Persians. The basic doctrine of the Olympic Games was declared after this victory. Essentially it was the elite or 'political class' who suffered in Greece. This must not be forgotten. Helots lived at the bottom of the social pyramid, like a less civilized version of serfs or slaves. Many were either artisans or laborers.

CHAPTER 4

Greek Mythology: Gods, Heroes, and Epics

Greek Mythology: Gods, Heroes, and Epics. The contest between gods and men is an aspect of ancient Greek mythology and literature, an ever-present theme, the struggle for human endeavor and a symbol for the ruthless politics of the time. The Greeks were certainly not one of those. From the earliest times, everybody loved to tell and listen to the myth; today, thanks to the theaters, we have much more poetic documents than we want them, and it is certainly not the case that the most were told were handed down in literature. Which shapes or gives form of his animism were in the human body? His anger, almost always the malignant malignant coat from the man, shows the poetic film to play. In the form of Mercury, others were jealous, wary, some others made him completely ridiculous. But all said or done on this bullet ball only admitted one thing: no one could believe that it was corning, that is to say, lie insipid! There was no other needy God who believed this, with the exception of the terrible Hero (mother Eris), to be a risk-free risk, and a man who did not believe in corruption.

Most of the Greek Judeo-Christian beliefs are in prime agony, with the back of the boat, for the sake of the strict Python rules, when the deceased pieces are set up to make the future of the Gospel not to make the future lucid half. The typical Greco-Latin giudaico-grammatical deus otiosus - yes, like the builders and the god of the couch, who is bored of lying lazy - lazy and palpant, tired, gratifies himself into one. During a more practical decline, desirous of sexual pleasure or coitus, he becomes incarnate and undergoes the technique of judging men, acting wisely, humane, and virtuously. Not like Jehovah, Allah, or similar gods, he is not a judge or a human being: on the contrary, a reduced flea, melancholic, with contemplation, who preys on squabbling.

CHAPTER 5

Crete: Minoan Civilization and Myth of the Minotau

Located south of the Aegean Sea at the southern end of the Balkan Peninsula, the island of Crete is famous for its history, civilization, and mythology. Crete, the place where the earliest European civilization flourished, had witnessed human activity as early as 7000 BC. The 3,000-year existence of the Minoan civilization in honor of King Minos of Crete is a notable part of its history. It is said to be named after King Minos. In Greek mythology, King Minos of Crete is a son of goddess Europa and Zeus.

The daughter of the king of Crete, King Minos, and Queen Pasiphae is loved by the sea god Poseidon. With the help of Poseidon, she gives birth to the Minotaur, a monster with the body of a man and the head of a bull. This beast is caged in a labyrinth, built by Daedalus, a master craftsman and architect. According to the myth, the Minotaur is said to be an annual sacrifice in honor of the gods. The hero Theseus sets out and slays the monstrous Minotaur in this labyrinth. In Greek mythology, Theseus is a legendary hero, responsible for the organization of many of the early Greek city-states. He traveled throughout Greece and the Aegean islands, uniting other city-states. He was responsible for the release of the young Athenians from Crete. He realizes that these young people are the holy sacrifices of the Minotaur and sends them on a ship to return to Athens.

CHAPTER 6

Santorini: Volcanic History and Myth of Atlantis

Santorini is one of the most famous and most visited islands in Greece, not least due to its gorgeous landscapes and stunning sunsets. Although it's often thought of as a single island, Santorini is actually a group of islands that were formed following a massive volcanic eruption in the middle of the Aegean Sea. Named Thira after the Dorian colonisers of the 9th century B.C., the island was the location of another major volcanic eruption in the 2nd millennium B.C. The eruption was one of the largest recorded and affected not only the island but devastated the Minoan settlements of Crete. Some believe that this surge of activity is what led to the creation and the association with the myth of Atlantis and the island of Santorini.

According to the myth of Atlantis as developed by the Greek philosopher Plato, Atlantis was a vast and advanced island nation that was at the center of an empire until it was destroyed and disappeared into the sea. There have been many locations suggested for the actual island of Atlantis, but the story of catastrophic volcanic eruption leading to a civilization's destruction is connected to the island of Santorini. Some believe that the myth of Atlantis is a heavily distorted version of a much earlier eruption on the island of Santorini, around 1600 B.C. In this model, the volcanic eruption on Santorini would correspond to the destruction of Atlantis. Plato stated explicitly that the story of Atlantis was quite wonderful to behold and well-attested in ancient legends. He presented it as a real place, offering precise details about city solutions and geographical descriptions. Santorini was a critical hub for Minoan civilization - an incredibly advanced and accomplished civilization.

CHAPTER 7

Rhodes: Historical Significance and the Colossus o

The town of Rhodes lies on the northeastern coast of the island, which is the largest of the Dodecanese (Southern Sporades), as well as the fourth largest island in all of Greece. It is a historic town and island that offers many attractions. Thucydides, the great 5th-century Greek historian, proclaimed that "...the island of Rhodes was inhabited by the Lose Greeks and by those who had come from Crete." Both Crete and the mainland of Greece are part of ancient Greek mythology – the Greek 'Religion' and the Great Pantheon of Athens. The island of Rhodes was a landen Minoa island located to the west of the Middle Eastern pantheon of gods. The town of Lindos on the Greek island of Rhodes – where the Colossus of Rhodes stood during the 3rd century – was occupied as early as the 4th millennium BC in the pre-Greek archaeological layer. The "Acropolis of Lindos" lies on a site that was held in "religious occupation" until 280 BC.

The Colossus of Rhodes was a monumental statue designed by the sculptor Chares of Lindos. It stood at the entrance of the Mandraki harbor, calling the Aegean sailors to "set course for imperial

Lindos," an ancient town on the island of Rhodes. Poets and the admiration of the ancients, as well as later authors, romanticized the details of the huge bronze statue to enormous and unbelievable proportions. Given the cost to create the statue and many inaccurate and sensational writings about it, many think the statue straddled the entrance to the Mandraki harbor, but that corresponds to the most likely real size of the original statue according to historians. The city of Rhodes (modern Ρόδος) is located off the southwestern coast of Turkey. It was famed in ancient times for both the island's agricultural products – figs, honey, wine, olive oil, and herbs. The island is still famous for preventers of "human deformity" – wine and sea breezes! It is also the place whereafter, "they filed out, in a Rapid of Rhodian Asmodei, both of gleaming bronze, the sculptured work of Lindian Menares."

CHAPTER 8

Mykonos: Modern Culture and Historical Background

Nestled in the sparkling Aegean Sea, the fairly slim island of Mykonos has developed a reputation for an all-hours party atmosphere. However, windsurfing fans flock here, drawn by the summer's meltemi (north wind), which helps keep temperatures mild. While Mykonos is indeed an island of no small size, locals were happy to show guests all over the island and its extraordinary beauty, incredible luxurious beaches, historical sights, and the areas of the mainland and the villages. The guests found the local customs, way of living, and farming of great interest.

Mykonos is well known for its energetic modern culture. The character and cause of this culture may be traced to various factors of its historical background, according to the current dominant mythology. Mykonos is believed to have been named after the demigod Mykons who some claim is related to the god Apollo. Thus begins the history and vital role of Mykonos in this sphere. It might have skipped a bit if we were to merely glance at the historical background. It was an island marvelously raw, almost deserted, and hard to travel when the history actually begins! Later, Mykonos became a significant weevil marketplace on the usual routes from the Republic of Venice, Europe, and Asia. In addition, many joined the Byzantine church of the island because it had to be officially proclaimed amongst the conquered land because of St. Panteleimon (for many years after being slid through the streets on a donkey, the saint was given an estate and a chapel on the island).

CHAPTER 9

Corfu: Venetian Influence and Mythological Connect

Though quieter and with fewer cultural attractions than the more popular islands to its south, Corfu (or Kérkyra, as it is known in Greek) has gained its popularity in more recent times, and underlying it is the island's interesting blend of landscapes, history, and mixed cultural influence - particularly that of Venice. It is less striking than its nearest neighbor, the Epirotes mountainous region and the Vikos Gorge, but its main city is well worth a visit for the blending of a series of architectural styles: Baroque, English, French, and Classical style. The wealth of vegetation has led it to being dubbed 'the garden', and the olive tree - valuable - and fruit are wild; Corfu is less Dalmatian than it is Greek as one would characterize it. The Ionian Islands, the most "western" of the Greek archipelagos, have long been the best known to travelers, a combination of their geographical-neurological position, their mild climate, and their deep historical connection to Western Europe as ("New Greece," as twelfth-century "Assassins" called them).

In the legend, Corfu is what became of the splendid ship that the Phaiatans presented to Odysseus, to take him back to Ithaca. Poseidon desired to chain the vessel to his island, and in its gold he found the gilding of the Athenian city's attack - which was coming to him - so he and Apollo sunk it before it ever landed on Phaiatia. This was accomplished; and, when one final passenger - Protheus' daughter, the runner of the sea, Thetis - asked to be set all alone on her own island before the ship was sent down to Poseidon, her request was granted. She returned home to rule alone or there; to marry her sea nymph, the fair "psalmist" (who also spent her girlhood at Protheus' court singing Psalms on behalf of her convent calling loudly for rescue) and rear a son, Iphtin (Ingel in English). It is closer still to the Albanian coastline, and shares many features with that country's seaboard. Corcyra or Corfu is mountains form most of its topography, with their heights providing fresh cooling breezes, and the water they are high enough to do either of two things when they spill into the sea: Force it into steep reed-filled platforms; or curl it.

CHAPTER 10

The Ionian Islands: History and Cultural Heritage

The history, culture, and civilization of the Ionian Islands, although supreme and ever-evolving in many ways, cannot be studied nor analyzed in complete isolation, outside of the context of the history, culture, and civilization of the rest of the Seven Islands and of the Eptanissa as a whole. The walls of nature, however omnipotent, will never be able to ponder and define the ultimate barriers of life, thus imposing artificial and temporary criteria which determine arbitrarily the individual nature and characteristics of each portion of the Seven Islands. Due to geographic peculiarities as well as the thirteen different chapters which make up their history, however, the Ionian Sea in which the Ionian Islands are located offers certain connecting points amongst floats, at the same time it segregates and cancels out the connecting factors of the geographical unity of the seven.

Prehistoric findings and inscriptions provide evidence that civilization on the Seven Islands began as far back as the fifth millennium B.C. during the Copper Age and the Bronze Age. In the section of land which the works of Thucydides and Livy called the

'Councer of the Ogygian Seven Islands,' developed the marine civilization of the Corcyreans co-existed with the newer institutions of Kephallenians. Close to Italy, amongst the Spartans, the Lefkadians were urged to lay down their laws and to establish a constitution by their founder, Laphias, who in so doing, sealed the statutory bond of the Eptanissi. Pictured illegibly from Troy to the last short military battle for Monemvasia, the Seven Islands were tossed about as spoils and war booty by the newcomers, each island constituting an object of exchange in the unspoken and written agreements. Oath-bound participant or not, no island had the good sense or ability to be true to its treaties, and a shameful role was played by either contention at the end of the day. The Seven Islands, though, were destined to change directions and coordinates. Talks began with powerful philanthropists who would offer their children in marriage here; old masters agreed and convened to give instructions while Eptanissi assassins revealed or concealed their backroom card game. When leaving, the game was to seat the competent and the no-goods on the Lefkada Table. An interesting blend of attitudes, if we take into account the fact that wherever a play disappointed its creators, octrois and passport controls dictated the terms of the game. In particular, within the confines of 'free hands' foreign powers in the Greek World apropos and declare in the heart of the confinements and Borghese sect. Flessian hands accuse the powers that be, that necessarily brought naval ships to protect the neutrality regency.

CHAPTER 11

The Aegean Islands: Historical Crossroads and Myth

The Aegean also cradles a number of islands, which the ancient poet Homer referred to as "teeming." The historian Herodotus of Halicarnassus claimed that there were around 3,000 islands in the Aegean; modern estimations have counted around 1,400-2,200, with the largest ones numbering at around 160 (for a combined area of 3,700 square miles). Today, the islands remain an important part of Greece's national economy, thanks to their beaches, agriculture, and, of course, the history stored within them. The heavier traveling months account for when Greek history-crafters and fans visit those islands in order to document the secrets that they may still possess.

The ancient model of the sea and islands being a collection of primarily small but manageable bits of land surrounded by a mostly unified body of water (the height of travel convenience, for the most part) has been in suspension in a modern world where information and transportation have developed far beyond the average human imagination. But the archipelago has been, and remains, the center of trade and commixture, of exploration and exploitation, of hatred and hospitality. The inhabitants of islands are as various as, if not more various than the islands themselves: the Casandralawn Cretans are religiously tolerant and beautiful but arrogant, just as the Rhodians are acquisitive and the populous of Mykonos are open to innumerable strangers, but xenophobically reserved toward mainland Greeks. Despite the apparent lack of "authenticity," what the islands provide in the way of historical record is usually so much culture/industry-mixed blood, and the question of the "authentic" whether concerning island culture or history can make no impression against the numberless layers of encrustation that have been laid down here over nearly five millennia of human tearing-and-rebuilding, or contrived peace-making, or other rare combinations of the first two. That's anti-historical; that isn't what we're trained to do. It's only a slight overstatement to say that you can find anything you want in the Greek islands, and the history of the Aegean so long as the Greeks haven't paved it over. The islands are everywhere in this regard part land, part sea, and all historic wasteland. A desert, or, rather, a waste.

CHAPTER 12

The Dodecanese Islands: Influence of Various Civil

Chances are high that the term "Dodecanese" is etymologically a Greek word. Dodeca in Greek means 12 while nisi means islands in the Greek language. The Dodecanese has been a Hellenistic land for much of its history. Minoan Crete is the first well-known eastern Aegean power that has links with the Dodecanese island cluster. The Dorians who came from the times of the late Bronze Age, i.e. 900-1100 B.C., were the earliest Hellenic tribe in the Dodecanese. The period of Alexander the Great and his offspring was the last time that the Dodecanese were under the control of a united political body. In 146 B.C., the islands were ceded to Rome, which allowed them to retain their freedom and authority as a subjugated city-state community.

The Dodecanese islands have always been under the influence of eastern Aegean wildlife, which has been cautious about Later Minoan Crete's immune policies. Full neolithic relics were found on Chalki island, also known as Khalki. These little Cyclades (a total of 24 such remote islands) were under Cretan prehistoric, (2000-1600 B.C.) a firm Cretan-Mycenaean cultural consort. In 1204, after the partitioning of the Byzantine kingdom in the wake of the 4th Crusade, the Dodecanese became the district of a Roman-League of Western Greece, which essentially Greekized the subsequent colonies. In the 11th millennium B.C., the first Greek-speaking herdsmen and groups of farmers founded residence on the islands of Nissiros and Kos. Until about 500 B.C., Christianity, which expeditiously became the dominant religion of the entire Aegean Sea, and became a province of the Byzantine empire of the Greek-Orthodox cardinates.

CHAPTER 13

The Cyclades: Ancient Sites and Mythological Stori

An exploration of the islands of the Cyclades, scattered across the Aegean Sea, their ancient sites, and their mythological stories. A famous wine was made on Lemnos, named Pramnios oenos derived from the smoky (pramnos) taste of the accidentally roasted grapes. Dionysos was very versatile apart from wine. In addition to sailors and vintners, he also protected the fertility of the vine. But other gods and heroes also had their sanctuaries on the islands.

The islands form an incomplete circle or "ring" (kyklos) around the sacred island of Delos, even then considered the central aeigilis or navel of the Cyclades. Today, Delos is a vast site - the only island where no one lives - still littered with broken statues, proving that this once tiny isle was also once of high importance in return for so few raw materials available. It was said to be sacred even from the ancient past by tour books of the time. An important historical site would have been fortified, giving vital protection to a promontory, the rate of a crossroads in the Aegean Sea.

CHAPTER 14

Delos: Sacred Island and Archaeological Marvels

In the heyday of ancient Greece, Delos was regarded as no less than the world's navel. Known to be the birthplace of Apollo and Artemis, it was for centuries the site of a major celebration of the gods. In our day, few not of the academic or Hellenophile persuasion can claim more than a fleeting knowledge of the island. The site is, in fact, an open-air museum, crammed with religious, commercial, and civic architecture from the eighth century B.C.E. right up to the late antique. In 1873, the French School of Athens started excavations on Delos, and the mission continues to this day, along with the excavation of the neighboring island of Rheneia.

The ancient Greeks believed that Delos had been infertile until the birth of Leto's twins. She gave birth under the branches of a palm tree on the banks of the Inopos River, where baby Apollo had a shady birth-cradle. The myth concludes with Leto bringing fertility and productivity to the island, and, thereby, making it a fitting place for the central panhellenic celebration Darieia, the early name of the festival held in honor of Apollo every five years. Delos is far more than an archaeological time capsule, however. Its sacred perimeter echoed proclamations in verse—some of which complement social-historical and religious information that was previously known or suspected from the plays and poems of the time. The statements also attest to the exceptional nature of the sanctuary. The terms used on the hymn can be interpreted theologically from the perspective of Apollo to mean the name and title, or authority, given by men to the god who approves and ratifies. At its heart was an immense, almost perfectly rectangular marble-paved platform covering 9500 square meters—more than two acres—originally enclosed by a portico. Inside this iconic sanctuary, religious personnel celebrated the hecatomb, sacrificing cattle, and composing and reciting hymns, songs, and flute music, with the greatest architectural marvels of the Greek world as a backdrop.

CHAPTER 15

Samos: Birthplace of Hera and Historical Importanc

The Greek island of Samos is set in the Eastern Aegean, and has been attracting tourists for centuries. Its white beaches and crystal clear waters make it a popular tourist destination. There are four cities on Samos, the most important two of which are the capital, Vathy, and Pythagorion. The latter is named after the Greek mathematician who was born on the island. Pythagorion was also the birthplace of the goddess Hera. In classical times, Hera was considered the protectress of the island. Before Apollo could take over the godhead, Hera could be found throughout the island in the form of birds. Colonizing Greeks, however, who were at odds with the fact that a woman was such a powerful force on the island, hunted the birds and killed them through the use of lime. In response to the desecration of their sanctuary, the goddesses of Samos fled to smaller islands in the vicinity.

The most important sight in all of Samos, the temple of Hera, was built in the seventh century BC; it was the largest sanctuary in Greece, covering an area of 500 hectares. As for the goddess herself, the temple is an emulation of other sacred lands, combining two other temples into one: the Ionic temple of Artemis of Ephesus of Anatolia (modern-day Turkey) and the Doric temple of Hera on the Argolid of the Peloponnese. The fifth century saw heroic effort in constructing the well-designed sacred road, 1.7m wide with on both sides of the large paved stones, about 3.5m long, with pyramidal tops. Throughout the Classical period, every building in the sanctuary was whitewashed, reflecting the evening sun with shimmering brightness. Inside, visitors to the sanctuary would make sacrifices to the goddess, dried figs and nice, big dates being particularly favored gifts. Perks of the temple also included a large water basin. However, today it serves as the residence for the tortoise ladies of Greece.

CHAPTER 16

Lesbos: Historical Legacy and Literary Connections

16. Lesbos: The historical legacy and literary connections of a Greek island

Lesbos, anciently designated by the names Lasia and Aiolia, has a long history with a population that takes pride in being Lesbians and has a well-documented contribution to the field of literature. The island, situated by the Lebanese mainland, houses two main cities of Methymna and Mytilene on both ends of the long island, each with its own proper history and current state of affairs. Lesbos has suffered from underdevelopment compared to the rest of Greece and has also been an undesirable place to settle in because of the harsh climate. The people of Lesbos have a rich tradition of literature, with many written accounts by those who were forced to emigrate due to its poverty.

The writers who most greatly influenced the development of modern Greek literature are Sappho of Eressos and her fellow-Islander, Alkaios. They had the ability to write in their local dialect and had a knowledge of world literature that is similar to the capability of a Roman poet to use Latin to write about local circumstances and concerns. Sappho has a generalized instead of even a timely quality. Lesbos is a barren and sparsely populated island off the coast of Greece, yet in the province of culture, it is almost an independent nation. It is the longing, as in the case with all individuals who long, practiced by all the well-to-do Lesbians who leave their country to live on the mainland to kill themselves over the impossibility of resting a few minutes while death approaches.

CHAPTER 17

Chios: Mastic Production and Historical Significan

Just about 7.5 miles (12 kilometers) from the Turkish coast, Chios is Athens's gateway to the Greek islands of the East. Chios is unique for its resins and mastic, the production of which was granted to the Byzantines in recognition of their assiduous attention to the protection of the grapes more suited to Naxos's volcanic soil. Chios was where the last Persian fleet defeated the Massaliotes in 394 BC. Inevitably, it felt the rough hand of the Romans, as testified by the ruins of the ancient city in its modern capital. There are still two forts in the small and steep medieval Mesta.

More major, the Genoese took the south side of the western bay with its Latin fortifications. A few days on Chios should give you time to travel about and enjoy the changing color of the weather—perhaps some of the irascibility transferred to the people who live far from the protection of the mainland. History is so full of the island that you will have no difficulty in finding places to explore on Chios. But be sure to acquaint yourself with the history and mythology of these islands before you set out.

Homer also provides us with a wealth of knowledge. Mastic was the ancient chewing gum and still grows naturally here. This is a tree resin that only Chios could produce. Mastic was used in Egypt, from whence it was sent up the Nile to the Nubians. In ancient Greece, it became famous under the name of "lentisk" in the time of their proverbial glory. Chios Island today has an area of 904 square kilometers but still remains mostly rural. This geographical region has seen steady growth throughout its entire history.

CHAPTER 18

Euboea: Second Largest Greek Island and Historical

Euboea is Greece's second largest island - and the lengthy yet narrow figure that it is (it stretches for about 150 kilometres/93.2 miles from north to south and with a maximum width of about 70 kilometres/43.4 miles), it is also the largest island of the scattered ones in the Sporades that run northwards along the coast of the region of the island-studded Aegean to the west of the Greek mainland. Over the centuries, Euboea has often been confused with Evia. The same confusion comes with the smallest of the main islands of this fluid archipelago. The larger of them is called Euboea, frequently spelled Evia, but officially inscribed as Euboia. Its main port to the north is called Histiaeia but, more commonly, Chalcis. The second largest island of Greece has been inhabited since the Neolithic era, with most of the settlement having taken place on the narrow coastal ranges in the north and the south - particularly of the latter where the major urbanized areas are to be found today.

Euboea has somewhat been overshadowed by its larger neighbor, and also, without a doubt, by its larger-than-life neighbor. Two of the nine muses were born on Euboea, as was Aristotle, Greece's most celebrated philosopher. By far the richest era for the island was the early Iron Age when the now overgrown Eretria of central Euboea was not only one of the wealthiest and most powerful settlements in Greece but the richest and most influential as Europe grew increasingly connected through wide stretches of middle humanity that reached far beyond the Mediterranean Sea into the northern Atlantic and down into the Indian Ocean to the south.

CHAPTER 19

Thasos: Ancient History and Mythological Links

A large emerald protruding from the emerald-clear water. This is Thasos, where technology and nature walk hand in hand. The numerous campsites and long sandy beaches contrast with the forests of pines and oaks that cover the mountains. The west coast is not very interesting, so the tours go east and terminate at Thasos Town. The ancient historical background of the city is of great interest. The Philippians founded it in 680 BC and were home to over 6000 people in their heyday. The gallery of lions with the heads of humans and the walls that wind down from the acropolis to the theatre are especially beautiful. Huge panoramas of the coastline are available at the sanctuary of Panagia. The villages of Marion and Limenas are also worth a visit. Thasos is in the northwest corner of Greece, about 8 kilometers from the coast of Eastern Macedonia. You must take a boat from Kavala to get there. Thasos Town is the most important city on the island, serving as the main port and connecting the island with the mainland by ferryboat.

On Thasos, the ancient history is alive. PAS is today the archaeological site of the ancient city of Thasos and has provided a great deal of information about the ancient populations of the northeastern Aegean Sea. It dates from 1616, which was AD. The theatre in the process, but still missing seats. Over the past decades, the theatre has hosted a number of dance, theatre, and musical events. The ancient marble quarry in Limenaria reveals that Thasos was prosperous in ancient times. The Sirens - who were supposed to reside on Thasos - could be found between Thasos and Limenas. Given the parallel between the name of the sirens, the Sirenum Cubital and one of the bays, the conclusion is well-founded. The cave of Panagia is in the town of Thasos. Fairly impressive, the cave indicates the intensity of the island's occupation. In Stones' watch, there is a monastic community in Saint Panteleimon at 250 m. The capital and largest town on the island is also known as Thasos. It is named after the ancient poet and traveler of the same title, who is said to have played a significant role in advocating for the island's deeds in the Argonautic epic of mythology. The online population of 3,0 suprepos is also only 188 km far from Thessaloniki, and just a half a kilometer from the mainland.

CHAPTER 20

Karpathos: Traditional Culture and Historical Root

Karpathos is the second largest island of the Dodecanese complex, with mountains, fertile valleys, and beautiful scenery on both its coasts. Olympos, in the north, is the island's main place of interest and has preserved many old traditions. Located near the island of Crete, Karpathos has been providing a homing place to various conquerors over the centuries who have all left their mark on the place.

The entire island of Karpathos remains remarkably unaffected by the passage of time. Karpathos is a living museum, reflecting the evolution of the Dodecanese Island customs and traditions of the times. The island also boasts magnificent scenery, superb sheltered coves, and wide powdery sandy beaches, plus an interesting history. The older villagers, over 60, who are increasingly scarce, are all fluent in their own dialect, which they speak between themselves. Knowledge of this dialect is certainly fascinating, entertaining, and full of color. They were raised in an era when there were few roads, no electricity, and no radio broadcasts. As far as tourism is concerned, Karpathos is still relatively unspoiled. It is a family island with an inquiring history as well as an inquisitive past that isn't completely set in stone. For history buffs, the cemetery located near the city contains countless Hellenistic kratères - strange handmade sarcophagi. Also worth a look is the church of Panagia Agèpté Rahtianì.

CHAPTER 21

Ikaria: Mythological Origins and Historical Develo

Ikaria, an island found in the northeastern Aegean Sea, has long been held in high regard. In ancient times, it was known for its fortitude, precisely because it was situated off the impracticable Leon range. Additionally, it maintained its independence during the centuries of Hellenic colonization and therefore earned a 'reserved underdeveloped area' reputation. It also preserved its knowledge for a long time after being conquered by the Romans. Because it was seen as rugged and unpromising, it was heavily populated by Roman refugees during the early Byzantine period. Ikaria, which is famous for its exports of silk and textiles, has been mentioned in international documentation several times. Additionally, it has been overrun countless times. Following the Greek War of Independence, Ikaria was included with Samos as a semi-independent administrative district and, in 1947, as a de facto federal region. Because the capital of Samos was in a poor state, the people of Ikari would not vote to unite on January 21, 1949, and instead voted to incorporate with its main island.

As far as the name of the island is concerned, it has been interpreted as either one that has been unclean or one that has been cost-free. Because Ikaria is referred liberorum by the Romans, it is widely thought that the latter term is the correct interpretation. The Proclus believed the island's mythical origin story was distinctive. According to him, Icarus, using waxed wings, anticipated the death of Minos, the King of Crete, who had fled to Ikaria after escaping from the Labyrinth. Sea sailors recovered the body of Icarus when it began to decay and prominent islands were thus given their title. Historically, "when Heracles was traveling from Sicily we learn that a large man named Thoas ruled the island in the time of Heracles." Inasmuch the Trojan War prompted the island to submit to Agamemnon. The Heraclid steps operated in Ioannis and Dracous simply change things because religion serves as more of an obstacle than a means to achieve success.

CHAPTER 22

Patmos: Religious Significance and Historical Even

'Explore picturesque islands, historic sites, and dramatic landscapes in Greece.' 'Start here: Travel to the Southern Mediterranean.' 'Don't leave Greece without checking out these islands.'

Patmos has a few religious significances, which is reflected in tourists, and the island's most popular aspect is the monastery and church of Saint John. Both were made in the 11th century A.D., with valuable books and icons. The islands were discovered by the Apostle John in 95-96 A.D., who also composed the Book of Revelation of the Bible. Exiled there for 18 months, he authored the book before being released and returned to Ephesus. According to mythology, he had deposed the emperor Domitian's order to murder him. A cave where the Apostle John resided can be visited by tourists, who will also find a number of religious icons present there. Emperor Domitian is also said to have erected a library, a temple, a stadium, and other amenities here, and that they were in use during subsequent Roman rule. During a visit to Saint John's Cave, you can still find the impractical vine of the Apostle John, which watered the meals of Domitian's meals.

Patmos played a significant part throughout the Cyclades' history. It was the primary base of Ionian Piracy during the 1st millennium B.C. In 479 B.C., the ancient navy of the Persian navy suffered a defeat during the battle of Lade. Patmos and Ionia were colonized by the Romans throughout the beginning of the 2nd millennium B.C. The name "Patmos" is a Latinized version of "Pati" (suffering) and "Soma" (body). It is said that St. John's exiled there experienced a cracked back. The island came under the control of the Byzantine Empire, where it was part of the Aegean Sea. In 1088 A.D., Christodoulos Ladias, the island's lord, constructed the older of Saint-John the Teolog. Fortifications were added to the two chapels within the monastery, there are valuable early Christian and Byzantine works of craft, and Thieves brotherhood are housed there. It is a site of worship as well as a high-quality tourist destination.

CHAPTER 23

Kos: Ancient Asclepeion and Historical Landmarks

The nearest island is Kos, which is, like nearly all the islands, mountainous, well cultivated and dotted over with towns and villages. At sunset, we move off to sea and steer for the island of Patmos. The ancient city of Kos was in the most ancient times called Meròpes from Meròpìs, the founder, who was the son of Æolus; in the Trojan time it was called Idòmes, and subsequently Lipso; whence came also Pœsas, the name of the river. But afterwards, accidentally, it was called Halasarna after the daughter of Meròpes; and at last Cos, either because its famous Asklepeions are fruitful in herbs and keep people well ("with food"), or after the diminutive cosìon given to the demigods.

The most important and interesting remains of Kos are, without doubt, the ruins of the Greek Asclepeion. One-third of which have now been excavated, the rest still lies unchanged amidst the dense wild fig, eucalyptus, and oleander. According to an ancient poet (Apolo. Bibl., xix, 5, 1), the worship of Asclepios first came from Crete to Izmiròi. In those times, the god of medicine and patron of the art of healing was worshipped under the form of a serpent (as of old in Atzmann). The staff of Aisculapius, serpent-entwined staff developed about 400 BC, is not to be found in the Cretan and early Carian sculptures. But about 300 BC, in the Canon of Polycletus, it is placed in the hand of Apollo, the son of Asclepios. Hence, the sanctuary of Asclepios at Kos, which is mentioned by the ancient writer 500 years before Christ, must have been founded about 2000 BC. The history of the Dorians in Kos is a history of unimportant events. Once Kos was sent to war as a Dorian colony, once its ten towns joined together to fight against a common local enemy: the people of Halikarnassos. When Alexander conquered Asia Minor, his admiral, Hegelochos, drove the Carian Byzantians across to Kos, about 2000 years ago. The Byzantine period lasted 800 years, longer therefore than either the Carians or the Ionians ever had. When Belisarius left Kos in the 6th century A.C., the time of antiquity began, for under the Byzantines Greece lay forgotten and surely covered up with mold.

CHAPTER 24

Andros: Maritime History and Mythological Stories

Andros - As high as 3,300 people lived in medieval Andros between the numerous settlements which are now ruins. Emporium of Minoan Crete, Andros welcomes traders ever since. Mycenaean architecture infuses variety into the country-house and flat-vaulted tombs (13th-8th c. BCE; Kyklades preprogrammed tour). From Minoan, Archaic and Roman Corinthian, Doric, and Ionic columns, Andriots pioneered Hellenism's most prolific investor nation. After the Roman civil wars, the victorious Keto all but annihilated the Greek trade fleet until the Cable Table, and its Minoan de-sand-banked harbour following the Second Ceylonism of 20 October 1969 intervened. Circa B.C. 111, a first oracle advised a heliographer: "Well built and unlikely, you can't die on high seas." Between 1300 and 1800, Andriote captains notched up three times as many hours at sea as the average Greek-motor Estimator family earns in a thousand years.

The tourist Effi Hofer (Strates, p. 342) misses Vedra, the cliffy miniature of Santorini. Some prefer the nag of the Schinoudaki cockerel. Authorities reckon that Schinoudaki littered Andros with

40 wind generators primarily in the excitement of saving Stavros-Cyclades from knob-galloping Maykres weeds. In the absence of an isopath Stavros-Stavros Airport, the clutter is already ruining tourism. In 220, the proliferation of choks showed no signs of abating, and efforts were being made to augment revenue where Panagia Theoskepasti, a pre-Metapolitefsi annual income of 11,188,000,000,000 was ranked first. A swamp, titled Kerato-trapeza, has emerged to the south sea's Siamese hike. If you stay the night in Chora (16), be sure to pierce Sinepolis. More vintage residences can be seen in Sineti and by the Jena route.

CHAPTER 25

Naxos: Myth of Theseus and Historical Sites

When Theseus left Crete and came to the island where his father had once held royal sway and sole dominion, and found the government and rule of the country shared equally between Nisos, already styled king, and his nephew Lykomedes, he concealed the royal title he had and went into their city as a stranger who claimed the hospitality which could not be denied. For he had left Crete without having taken any vessels with him, therefore he was forced to succumb to the hands of strangers.

Theseus succeeded so far in winning the good graces of Lykomedes that he introduced him to his daughters and told him by a sign, neither incautious nor difficult to observe, they would be able to tell what he must do in order to return home sound and living. Jam bread should in every matter of treat and action keep hidden the most exquisite ruling force on Naxos.

Then the island was first settled, and the settlers raised a temple and dug a trench and built an altar to Apollo, on which were set up four images of the god, looking the four different ways of the winds.

Naxos, the largest of the Cyclades, still wears a more genuine smile on its troubled face than any of them. Its story is much the same as that of the sister islands, but it has more interesting scenery—a truly glorious confusion of hill and valley, great cliffs chiseled into picturesque precipices, all ablaze in the morning and evening with the warm bronze light of the southern sun.

The whole island is like a half-famished mother holding out a starving child to some beneficent uncle and saying, "Now, if we can only get something out of him, we shall be all right!" Once upon a time, Ariadne came here with Theseus, and here, according to some traditions, he left her asleep on the shore and went away and never returned. It is also said that the vessel, after leaving Crete, was so crowded on board that she was forced to land here, and the place on the island where the unhappy lady was stayed behind has ever since been called by her name. In historical times, it was a Cretan colony and one of the stations for the triremes of Athens in the Archipelago.

CHAPTER 26

Paros: Marble Quarries and Historical Heritage

The third largest island in the Cyclades, the island of Paros, is famous for its special marble which is used to create cheap, bright, traditional church and house art. It is also known for its world-famous unique ancient sculptures made with Parian marble. One of the largest tombs in ancient Greece was discovered on Paros. There are many churches built in the Aegean architectural traditions.

The biggest and most fertile valley of a single island in the Cyclades is called the "Aspropotamos Plain" (Marathi meaning). It is said that the olive trees, from the Mycenaean period to the present, do not belong to the Greeks but were brought to Greece by the Arabs. These olive trees have acquired the title of "superior olive oil location" due to their own special anatomical features. During that time, cold storage technology was applied to ensure that the olive oil would not go bad. In the old days, pottery and ceramics contributed to the island's economy by selling goods. However, the product distribution was limited to nearby islands such as Naxos, Sifnos, Sikinos, Amorgos, Antiparos, Folegandros, and Santorini.

Daylight tours of ancient and modern quarries: The ancient quarries are located 10 kilometers south of the city's main harbor, east of Amoni or Marmor, Tzane or Tingion. The ancient name for this area was Mount Marathami. There are standard transportation facilities available, including accommodation, excursions, taverns, and catering services. The Tsanis or Tzane quarries have the same characteristics as those in the Tzane region. The area also hosts a traditional village with small and medium-sized fortress churches. It is located between Marpissa and the Tsujia painters of Naoussa. This area has been declared a purely traditional settlement and has a great historical heritage.

CHAPTER 27

Serifos: Mining History and Mythological Legends

Just 11,008 people, according to the latest survey, inhabit the small island of Serifos. For thousands of years, the development of the small island was dominated by its rich mines. The lifestyle on the island was reserved by the mine and have fun working, often the women environmental workers. All forms of respect all over the world Sen's mythology well-known island. The Greeks have any song referring to it. One of the most famous inhabitants of the island was a mentalist saint named Ai Gais. The saint was the island's hermit and at the same time he dealt with magic. During World War II, the Germans forced locals to work in Niatsio, a concentration camp. Besides the rich history of the Serif of Folklore Museum, there is also the lighthouse of St. George on Tzanes, the church of Agia Triada in Krio, and the monastery of Strouma, of course.

Serifos in mythology was also known as the island of him. It is in the world of Ai, namely god Hypocrites, as the ancient Greeks called this corner, all seekers of escapism. A place known to Grinder can make only one shade of the island white. If the shadow of the plants is red. The mountains hide necessarily large underground wealth.

The underground material was given to him by Danos, the first population of Greece to become a mine priest in a blossom mine (modern Zeus's cave), midway between Plateau Skia and the entire chain factory. Danes were established with island resettlement, Bello, and Sussi. A giant, in particular, was riding a pirate on Baros. The island has had legendary wealth ever since. Much later, pigs, sons of the late kingdom of Ceramic, lived in the Tinian harbor of Aé. A Deucalion saved by the flood of carnivorous and elation to the top of the rock, relieving the Pallan as air escapes. And since that time Pournos enjoyed his mythological jams. It is said that Perseus, the son of Zeus and Danni, was waiting in the armament factory for the weapon for the intervention of the winged ones, from the island of the Armenian necklace. This was where Perseus accidentally freed Andromeda from the ground snake. Altar Island.

CHAPTER 28

Symi: Architectural Beauty and Historical Importan

Symi is a beautiful island washed by many years of foreign conquests and the harsh Dodecanese climate. From the Middle Ages to the Archipelagos sea, it was a rocky, uninhabited island that was often used as a pirate base. But, from "koukoumesses" it became a great force with its shipyards, and its prosperous people dominated the entire region. Symi - Yio, grandmother is the granddaughter of Apollo. The name Yimokratara indicates the island position - name of, the French adopted it in 1365 and the Venetians, after taking the island in 1421, corrupted the name as Sims. In Turkey, the Greeks retained the corrupted name and lived in Sims until 1912. The Turks modified the name Yim into Turkish and sounded as Sym.

Symi's architecture is a reflection of the prosperity of its inhabitants throughout the 19th century and, combined with its beauty, captivates all who visit it. To visit the Metropolis Square (or Nimborio for the locals), one must follow the narrow streets up to the top. Here we meet the main church of the island's capital, St. John Theologos of the 19th century. Symi also has Byzantine churches and chapels of unique architectural interest. In the past, in the old town, temples could be found in every corner. 70 in total. During the 19th century, the vast majority were abandoned or altered. Today, there are 110 to 120 temples. In the city you will find the house/museum of the famous musician, Michail Kalogirou with his tools. Symi gave birth to not only people who built, but also people who sang and sang a lot of good things. Symi has fostered an influential musical tradition with good singers and composers outside. Builder Leonides Zahoulis, filmmaker Nikolas Kalopedis, singer Anastasis Sakellaridis. Symi took the tradition and sang for 21 years. Symi spoke and said something about the daily life of the active next door.

CHAPTER 29

Kythira: Venetian Influence and Mythological Tales

Kythira, once upon a time the harbor of Sparta, is an admirably convenient name for Ithaki. Father Time has seen to it that this island does not have more than 1,500 inhabitants today. Here, the lord of Odysseus, Tyndareos, was married to Harmodia, the sister of Kyperous. That great Venetian poet, Petrarch, wrote some verses in praise of the island. The Venetians would have liked to come closer to it, and during the Venetian domination of about 400 years that lasted from the 13th to the 18th centuries, they built strong garrisons on the rocky forts. They also built the palace of the Kytherian Despotess, entirely surrounded by cypresses, which served as a barrier between them and the people they had subjugated. Yeneyeni, Kythiraki lalusse, slow pace to counteract fast-to-go.

Many of the people of Kythira maintain that the sea forms a curve between Kythira and Crete that forms a grave. From long ago, even before this curve formed a grave, people from Crete crossing on passage boats of spruce wood or cedar through the breeding places used to be seen arriving there at Kythera where they would bury their dead and then leave for Crete again. And this is the reason those places, being the breeding stations of that passage through, were named "Boiotian Akrae" (the Cretan Begids). The memorial stele inscription from 1354 BC states: "Beautiful Kythera, with wide straits in front of you and fair temples inside". Most of the inhabitants of the island are Hellenes from the Peloponnese.

CHAPTER 30

Hydra: Maritime Tradition and Historical Backgroun

In Greek, Hydra island literally means 'water.' It is going to tell us that the ancient people of the Aegean believed in one of the myths. As the myth goes, according to the ancient Aegean seamen, dolphins often appeared in the sea around the island of Hydra, which seemed to hover in the sunlight and shadow in the sparkling bright silver sea. In view of the fact that all ages have lived on this sea, from ancient times to the present day, the Greeks have confirmed in many senses the idea of the immortality of the sea, even in the ripples of water.

Throughout history, the general Hydriots began to rule the Greek war of independence during the Ottoman corvée period from 1460 to 1821. Basically, the population developed Hydra for its dockyard's maritime trade. The Athens metro of which is the closest in Peiraias. The islanders were secluded from tourism by waving modernism in the Inner Sea world between Aigina and Poros but also by shaking western royal travel to the Ionian cities of Pavel and Ithaca. It is interesting to note that the port of Hydra is the highlight of the big rivers that lie studded with many landslides on the eastern

Aegean Sea, namely, and western part of the Peloponnese. Also, the Greeks introduced the horsepower of the hydra as the first artificial change in the Aegean Sea during the 1920s. The "horsepower" that has been raised to move the mule. Therefore, the event of horse racing is still planned every four years, to be held in the late part of June in the cost of Hamlet's journey.

CHAPTER 31

Skopelos: Natural Beauty and Historical Significan

S kopelos is part of the Sporades group of islands, which lies in the northwest Aegean Sea and is part of Greece. It is located north of its nearest neighboring island, Euboea. The terrain consists of green mountains with cliffs that meet the sea, green forests, and azure blue water. It is an archipelago and a major historical site dotted with ancient ruins and citadels. The island of Skopelos was actually part of the first Ancient Greek civilization. The cities of Skopelos and the islands of Euboea and Skopelos were established as independent Greek states. It's no wonder that there is so much history on such a small island. With a maximum speed of 45 km/h, it is possible to get around the entire island in less than 2 hours. The island's beaches are some of the only ones in the Mediterranean that are not surrounded by enormous hotel buildings. All of the shore is clean and undeveloped, with the only signs of civilization being the restaurants and taverns.

One of the best sites to see in Skopelos is the old town, perched right by the coast. It has the largest citadel in the Greek islands, which has been reconstructed largely thanks to the Ancient Greek tourist board. Skopelos has a long history dating back 1600 years.

Aside from the survival of the Dark and Medieval Ages, the Byzantine churches have been preserved in the old town. Other sights you don't want to miss are the Ecclesiastical Museum located in the grounds of the 10th-century church of Panagitsa tou Pyrgou. The museum houses some beautiful artifacts, such as ecclesiastical silk embroidery and Byzantine icons. Also, worth seeking out is the Folklore Museum at the port of Chora. It's housed in a handsome, traditional stone mansion, and has some interesting exhibits celebrating local crafts, traditional costume, and the art of traditional musical instrument-making.

CHAPTER 32

Kefalonia: Stunning Landscapes and Historical Even

Kefalonia has stunning landscapes and is a destination that attracts romance with its exuberance. The island has unique points that should not be missed. The most famous of these is Drogarati Cave and Lake Melissani. The underground lake Melissani, surrounded by a forest, offers a dazzling spectacle. The shades of green, turquoise, and blue in the region provide a magnificent view. In addition, an ancient fishing village named Assos, 40 kilometers from Argostoli, stands out with its colorful houses and turquoise sea. Antisamos, which is a breathtaking beach, and mountainous Poros Villages are among the regions that should not be missed.

The island is also home to a number of unique species, the most impressive of which is the Caretta-Caretta turtle. After mating, the mother turtles lay their eggs in the Kefalonian Turtles Protection Bay. Cape Skopos in the south of the island offers an excellent opportunity to see these turtles. Although the movie Myrtos Beach, famous for its sea and coastline, is often referred to as the island, its temperament has attracted attention to Pyrgi. In recent years, the coast, where the cypress trees grow, was reviewed in Captain

Corelli's Mandolin. The love story that started during World War II has touched people's hearts around the world. The makeshift house and beautiful village in Duvalata are a special place where thousands of visitors flock every summer. St. George Castle near Peratata, St. Andreas Monastery in Ano Drong and Drota Venetian Water have been spared from ancient times to guide us on the island.

CHAPTER 33

Zakynthos: Shipwreck of the Panagiotis and Histori

Zakynthos is a Greek island located south of Kefalonia, also within the Ionian Sea. Famous for its breathtaking landscapes, it has a humid subtropical climate. The eastern two-thirds of the island is quite hilly, and it does not experience heavy snowfall. The island offers striking mountain ranges, beautiful sandy beaches, warm Ionian Sea waters, lovely bays and coves, and lush vegetation. There are lots of things to do in Zakynthos, as it is rich in history. It is home to around four museums and two major historical sites for tourists and history buffs to explore and discover. Its long history includes periods of Mycenaean, Ionian, Greek, Byzantine, French, Turkish, Italian, British, and German rule. The shipwreck of the merchant ship Panagiotis is part of its modern history. With a predominantly shipping industry, tourism, and agriculture, improving an increasingly fading lemon production, the island still struggles to be self-sufficient.

Zakynthos, also known as Zante, previously called Fioro di Levante, is a sunny island in the Ionian Islands of western Greece. The island's historical background extends far back from the 20th century onwards; once it was referred to as Zankle (Scythe), either because of the shape of the land or from the lazy lifestyle of its inhabitants who used their scythes for settling disputes. Homer believed that Zakynthos was founded by Zakynthos, son of the King of Elean, Dardanos Ageno, and it was mentioned in two famous ancient tales. The first tale was the abduction of Zakynthos and his companions by Etruscan pirates, who worshiped the goddess Venus. They landed on a deserted island when Zakynthos promised to build her a temple in order to dive in her hometown as she wanted to bring them out from starvation and homelessness. Around 453 BCE, the Peloponnesian and Messenian colonial period was marked by Zakynthos.

CHAPTER 34

Lefkada: Myth of Sappho and Historical Legacy

Lefkada, just as the cave of the Nymphs in which it lies, as well as many other places around the world, are inextricably entwined with myth and reality, poetry and history, natural beauty and civilization, as well as symbol and substance. The myth of Sappho takes place, along with the related myth of Phaon, on the neighboring island of Zakynthos; nonetheless, archaeological evidence suggests that within the cave of the Nymphs there was also a cult of Aphrodite, parallel to the initiation rites practiced by girls entering adulthood. Its geological and paleontological features are also fascinating: the cave's impressive formations and the subfossil finds of an ancient hippopotamus, a pygmy elephant, and many other mammals are targets of ongoing research and are shown to the public upon request. In the vicinity of the cave, archaeologist J. Megas located a sanctuary of the Nymphs dating back to the Early Roman Era.

Lefkada: the myth of the island found in the works of the artists and poets of the ancient world - just like Zakynthos, Ithaca, and other locales surrounded by the Ionian Sea - is said to have forever inspired Homer and Lefkadian Sappho. Distinguished from her namesake, the fragmentary voice of the Lefkadian island-woman whose vivid, poetic life is beautifully portrayed by the local museum's bronze statue, the same as may have been crafted by the Chian Perillos, established a series of six dialogues, men, the only direct evidence for this from the Classical Era. Lefkada did, indeed, have an island sanctuary and a summer festival with competitions, but it is certainly not a sure thing that Sappho attended. A lengthy and complex history surrounds the island and its namesakes throughout the ancient period, the Medieval Era, and the Renaissance.

CHAPTER 35

Amorgos: Cultural Heritage and Historical Developm

Amorgos. At the 2011 census, the population was 1,973 inhabitants, and its surface is 121 km2. The geological-historical development of Amorgos follows the geological-historical development of the rest of the insular complex of the Aegean. The island of Amorgos is characterized by its cultural heritage, and the island comprises characteristic landscapes such as agricultural terraces with perennial olive groves and lofts, the historical network of footpaths and rural/agricultural buildings and settlements, the main coastal features with the harbor settlements of Katapola, Aegiali, and Arkesini, and the slopes or certain beaches of mainly wild landscapes with natural elements in a near-natural state. The land-use in Amorgos is primarily the product of abundant landforms rich in andesite and marble. The main, once until the 1960s, export items from Amorgos were marble and whetstone. Amorgos has two main harbors: Katapola in the southeastern part of the island and Ammoudi at Aeigiali bay in the northeastern part of the island.

The economy of Amorgos is quite different from the rest of the Cyclades. Amphorisms, the region of Arkesini (close to Aegiali), is famous for its ancient quarries for the extraction of marble and stone vessels (the amphorisms). In Greek mythology, Amorgos or Amolgos was the legendary island of the gods where they kept the wind immured. Amorgos hosted, in the Early Cycladic period (3rd millennium BC), early settlers, and then Amorgos became part of the Cretan-Minoan civilization. Over time, Amorgos experienced similar historical development to the rest of the Aegean until its occupation by the Romans. The Byzantines conquered the island in 1210 AD when the hill of Chora was fortified, and now the ruins can be seen. After several administrative changes, the current communities of Amorgos belong administratively to the Aegean Regional Administration, which is technically the region of South Aegean. This project action focuses on the portrayal of the historical development of Amorgos during the past 4,000 years and provides a rough overview of its frequent changes in the settlement areas.

CHAPTER 36

Ithaca: Homer's Odyssey and Historical Background

I thaca is an island of emerald lushness and remarkable beauty referred to by Odysseus's faithful servant and friend, Eumaios. Few general literature readers know that Odysseus's homecoming is a fundamental piece of epic in world literature, that The Odyssey is a work. However, few people understand that "another" modern word, Ithaca, refers to a very small group of islands in the Ionian Sea, not far off the western coastline of Greece, which goes back millennia. In fact, if Homer, who appears to have written The Odyssey in the 8th century B.C., was even a true figure in history or just a legendary character, the story of apparently his own island, Ithaca, would be intimately connected with his well-known text. Thus, Ithaca's literary and metaphorical significance goes even further than its natural and historical significance. This modern "Ithaca" is only about one eighth the size of Long Island, which is where New York City "is" in the U.S.A. The modern Greek island of Ithaca is also a few square miles of Mediterranean greenery and beaches that tourist organizations all over the world promote as "absolutely beautiful."

The island of Ithaca, off the west coast of Greece, plays a central role in Homer's tale of Odysseus's despondent homecoming after having survived the Trojan War. Thus, the literary and historical significance of Ithaca goes back well over three millennia. In Book Fourteen of Homer's Odyssey, which was composed in the 8th century B.C. (or even earlier), the swineherd Eumaios asks the disguised Odysseus where he comes from, and he answers: "I am from Alybas or maybe Epirus, either place or Crete, and I am the bearer of round-about damage because the wind drove me from Ithaca" (XIV.191-95). A few hundred years before Homer, Mycenaean Greeks seem to have settled Ithaca, although it is obvious from the many post-Homeric periods of conflict on the island that disputes for control of the land (over poor "rulers," or basileis) were likely fought out over many centuries across the ages. For modern Ithaca was hardly Odysseus's Ithaca, and there are numerous historical facts and arguments to support this astonishing claim. In his famous ge-ography, Book I, Herodotus (the so-called "father of history") lists Ithaca (Ithaka) as one of the seven Ionian islands, "whose barbarous inhabitants were formerly Cephallenian mountain bandits. The is-landers who had gone to Delphi to bring gifts for the Pythian games, in making a journey of supplication, complained to the Amphicty-onic Council that the Cephallenians had plundered them." In 1089, in fact, the Byzantine Emperor Alexius I Comnenus did "recover" the island from a local tyrant named Michael Maurelates, who was appealed to for help by the Kefallonians. Evidently, the modern Greek myth of Ithaki being the center of Odysseus's realm had not been invented by that time, or Alexius would likely not have listened to the Kefallonians.

CHAPTER 37

Paxos: Olive Oil Production and Historical Signifi

A history of continuous olive oil production and annual agricultural events, Paxos is also mentioned in Homer's Odyssey, hosting the mythical Odyssean monastery of Paleokastritsa on its western shore. The tiny island of about 2500 inhabitants is cloaked in olive groves, vineyards, and Mediterranean maquis, and encircled by a turquoise sea grazing the sheerness of its flanks. From the tiny, weathered port of Gaios, you can explore the sea caves of the small islet of Mongonissi by boat or amble around on foot to take in the architectural detail of Greek houses built on Venetian ruins and with doors tall enough for the local man's pointy black hat. In the dry mountain paths above the villages, there is the Crostatea nearby, a breezy terrace where you can sip drinks, listen to classical music, and admire the view of Corfu and of the curious Erimitis sandstone with its open cave. Around 100 holy sites are scattered over Paxos; of these, the early Christian Basilica of Ayios Apostoli on the coast of Longos, converted from a Hellenistic house in the 4th century, has been fully excavated and restored. Further along the coast road that loops around the island, time-worn churches often cling scenically to cliffs that look over the sea. You can hop between Paxos and Antipaxos by regular boat, hire a kayak or pedal boat, or wind, paddle, or sail your way between the tea green water and the seashore.

The oil has been produced since antiquity and is a dark emerald-green, acidic in its youth and as smooth and golden as honey after a few months. In October, the villages celebrate the olive press and the last quarterly, and many eyes look towards a traditional stampede that was originally intended to celebrate 1854 taxes: wine barrels were emptied from the Paladio cliffs and ran into the sea to avoid tax payments; on Paxos, the tradition continues, and the colorful procedure in coffee, animal festivities, and finally islanders at sea festively with the free wine. Olive oil has fostered Paxos' ancestors, the Giants of ancient mythology whom legend claims named the islands and expelled the God Poseidon from their shores when in a fit of pique he tried to alter the course of a river which they employed for irrigation. In Cleopatra's age, the Roman governor of Corfu imported the 'per pure' oil to a palatial oliterion overlooking the ancient town of Kassiope.

Today, the villagers generously empty the contents of their private olive trees into the presses of the island's only olive oil factory so that Corinthians, black or red (depending on the mix of British influence, world crop yields, and local humor) or harvest equal, can be produced and ready for tasting by mid-December.

CHAPTER 38

Antikythera: Ancient Shipwreck and Historical Disc

The legend of the Titans suggested that Antikythera and Kythera were thrown to separate their power. Antikythera produced the finest honey and its name evokes myth, beauty, and nature. Every sunset and when night falls, music is produced, a sound that is heard by swallows alone. In an effort to find meaning in the myriad artistic representations, interpretations of the Antikythera shipwreck and the mechanism attempted to interpret and explain. Antikythera's historical significance as an ancient shipwreck is central to this study. What convinces you to love this topic for your BA thesis? What do you know about Antikythera's historical significance and archaeology? The shipwreck and its surrounding outputs are examined in Antikythera in connection with Antikythera's ancient site.

The Cleveland Museum of Art studies the extended archaeological work of the Antikythera field to present the most detailed study of the Antikythera wreck's context, site, and historical dimensions. The analyses in this volume are based on fieldwork and studies of the Antikythera shipwreck documents in the archives of the

Ephorate of Underwater Antiquities in Athens. Our research extends the archaeological field to include economic and environmental (geomorphological), biological, historical, and long-term nautical aspects, emphasizing the importance of tools and methodology used in the analysis of original research data. Until the mid-February 2014 field season, the latest data from the Cleveland Museum of Two are presented, contradicted and joined by data from other research in the Antikythera shipwreck.

CHAPTER 39

Kythnos: Geothermal Springs and Historical Backgro

Although it hasn't figured significantly in any key historical event, Kythnos plays a role as the first island mentioned by Homer in "The Odyssey," where he tells a story about the hero-king Oileos, who lived on the island ruled over by the wonderfully lavishly wealthy king Aithon. He does not reveal the exact location, but researchers found some interesting details. It seems that ancient tomb hunters scoured the island looking for King Aithon's gold! Multiple finds and artifacts, especially Mycenaean ceramics, bear witness to the Minoan, Mycenaean, Geometric, Classical, and Hellenistic reflections of its cultural wealth. The most significant ancient evidence is considered to be the double-faced herma depicting Kaviras, the cult deities of the Kavirian Mysteries.

Founded in the 18th century BC, Kythnos flourished during the third millennium BC, developing into the wider Cycladic society. Kythnos had relationships of friendship and rivalry mainly with Kea and then with Melos, and in the sixth century BC, it came under the control of Athens. Shortly thereafter, the islanders refused to participate in the campaign against Cyprus and mobilized a Thasian fleet to free themselves. In 146 BC, Kythnos was involved in Roman-Ptolemaic disputes in Eretria (old Kese). In the ensuing centuries, Kythnos experienced periods of prosperity as well as depopulation, raids by pirates, as well as at least one attempt to use the island as a botanical garden. During the War of Independence (1821-1822), Kythnos was plagued with disease while famine struck the whole country. In 1855, it was hit by an earthquake that caused damage, resulting in the renewal of Byzantine baths built by the Turks.

CHAPTER 40

Skiathos: Beaches and Historical Landmarks

With an area measuring just 50 km², the most famous of the islands of the Sporades is a green island, adorned with 60 beaches. It is a real paradise for those who love the sun and the sea. If the southern part of the island is steeper and wilder, the northern part is more inhabited and well-hidden behind the thick vegetation on the hills. Skiathos is also its capital, that is to say the tourist pole, and opposes its historical position.

Nautical centre par excellence, it has a port on the Aegean Sea, formed with three entrances in a slightly calmer sea – the latter is a true natural spectacle. In this paved white city, the small houses are covered with red tiles and are decorated with bright red and blue shutters. A city which is mainly noted for Saint Nicolas Church, an ancient basilica whose ruins stand out in the middle of flowers. And it is also there, bathing in the heart of the city with its walls of the Venetian period, that we find the remains of the fortifications of Bourtzi. Above the bay entrance to the city, the Fortress of the Paliohora dominates, built over a prehistoric acropolis. Further afield, the island's museums offer the opportunity to explore the rich historical heritage and mythology of the Greek islands.

CHAPTER 41

Alonissos: Marine Park and Historical Significance

A lonissos is one of Hellenic Seaways' stopovers during the Thessaloniki-Sporades ferry route and bears the title of the Sporades' marine park. Alonissos and the other northern Sporades islands, in general, tend to be the first choice among swimmers, passionate fishermen, and divers directly from Thessaloniki and nearby regions. Moreover, the island has undergone significant construction development in recent years, especially in the Old Village area (Palaia Hora), because the locals have been breaking down their old family houses and rebuilding them stone by stone, making them look new. The Cycladic house architecture in Palaia Hora is less obvious than in other Greek islands but is most emphasized and can be located closer to the southeastern end of the village, near the church and elementary school. The western part of the island, the Cape to the south, has a unique geomorphology and offers breathtaking landscapes and unique opportunities for exploring—to tell the truth, part of the area is within the elementary school of St. John the Theologian, so access is not allowed during the academic year.

The coastlines of Alonissos and Central Greece are connected by culture and present the same geomorphological architecture, which is detailed in the work of Pausanias, Portal of Antiquity. According to mythology, Alonissos was, in the time of the Argonauts, already inhabited by Cretans and Pelasgians. In all likelihood, the island was inhabited during the Mycenaean Age, as evidenced by archaeological findings in Cavo Mourtias. It suffered only a few pirate invasions, gaining great commercial importance. In the Medieval Era, the island was given by the Byzantine Empire to the Ottomans. The beginning of the 19th century was marked by the Russian-Turkish wars, and the number of monks at the Monastery of Holy Pelagia dropped drastically.

CHAPTER 42

Tinos: Religious Pilgrimage and Historical Importa

Tinos - Locals affectionately refer to the winding lanes and glaring-white structures of the 194-square-kilometer Tinos as "the street of the Venetians." This large island to the northwest of coast-deep Syros was settled as early as the sixth millennium BCE. Heliacal luxation converts it into a religious pilgrimage every year, attracting thousands of attendees from around the globe. Religious services in both Greek and English are presided over by members of both churches, albeit the sanctuary honors the "Visitation by Mary to Elizabeth." Pilgrims, often refugees fleeing war-torn homelands, call the bell-rope handles that hang from every wall, creating an anvil chorus. The challenged fulfill a promise made to Mary, and the grateful contribute new ones for delivering them. We also saw dozens of crutches leaning against the rear wall, abandoned by formerly lame pilgrims.

Tinos holds a significant place in modern Greek history for another cause, besides faith. Tinos Chief of Police Konstantinos Kozadinos delivered Greece to the Allies during World War II. He related how, as he gave the 77-word notice to the teletypewriter operator at the Ministry of the Interior on September 7, 1944, an officer removed his gun and told him he was under arrest. "Go ahead and arrest me," replied Kozadinos. "I have already sent the message." Germany had occupied Greece for five years and two months, that evening. According to myth, the Amphitriti, the sea goddess Themis, gave birth to the wind god Aeolus at Cape Exomvou, eroding the earth that joined Tinos and Mykonos in two hours. Locals constructed the Sanctuary of Poseidon to commemorate Aeolus' entry into the world. In 2006, 350 vintage inscriptions honoring the god of the sea were uncovered in a sunken pile of Accra Donald and Gillian Borus' findings offer evidence of metallurgy, trading, and socioeconomic stratification on an ancient sea output site here.

CHAPTER 43

Koufonisia: Small Islands and Historical Backgroun

Greece is the perfect June travel destination. The spirits are high, the weather is beautiful, and there is no shortage of things to do on the islands. Most areas of Greece have returned to normal life following the international travel shutdown, demonstrating the spirit of the Greek people to continue living and see their beautiful nation thrive. The islands may be in turmoil, but the Mediterranean is as welcoming as ever in the week after European travel restrictions have been reduced and nations like the UK, Slovenia, Italy, and France have opened their doors to tourists. Here, we will be discussing the small islands of Koufonisia and Serifos to show you a corner of Greek modern history and the beauty of the Greek islands.

As far as we can tell, the islands of Koufonisia (plural) were named after the hollow caves located at the base of the cliffs on the shore that were designed for harvesting onions. Others believe that the islands, which provide no natural shelter for mariners, were blasted by speakers who used the loud boom of sea urea inside to deter seafarers from shipwrecking on the coast. As Eleftherotypia writes, Koufonisia is a small but well-organized archipelago made up of the Pano Koufonissi (Upper Koufonissi) and Kato Koufonissi

(Lower Koufonissi) islands. The Church of the Virgin Mary of the Rosary stands in the courtyard as a testament to the conquest of the tiny island by pirates. These wealthy islands on the southern coast of Naxos were first inhabited around the 4th century BC. They are near the mouth of the Cave of Zeus, which shows a wide range of vases and other objects used for religious ceremonies.

CHAPTER 44

Conclusion: The Enduring Legacy of Greece's Island

As much in the ancient world as in the modern one, Greece is defined not only by its islands and its mainland, but by the peculiar and circular relationship between them. Islands are internally divided by their mountain ranges and peninsulas, and surrounded by smaller islands. Their coastlines are utterly irregular, composed of an endless series of bays, capes, and promontories. These coasts encourage a lookout to the sea, forcing island and mainland settlers alike to become voracious sailors and builders of ships from the earliest time onwards.

The scholar Polynē (of the so-called Homeric Hymn to Apollo) visits the island of Delos precisely at the time its inhabitants are busy trying (unsuccessfully) to change their bays and harbours from artificial to a more natural lie-of-the-land, and is struck by the circular impossibility of this activity. And so, any effort to describe the history and mythology of the Greeks shortly ends up imitating this peculiar circular incursion.

We set out this beginning of the present volume with the ambition of describing some fifty or so of these Greek shorelines and inlets – not with the kind of geographical or nautical focus that can stress the sharp specificity of any one coastline against the flat blackness of the undifferentiated sea, but rather with the kind of textual multiplicity that might stress their essential sameness. Somewhere in between somewhere and nowhere, then, Greek histories and Greek mythologies seem forever to return back onto themselves, almost chasing themselves around and around any circular coastline until their shape is lost out of pure exhaustion. This volume then has turned out to work in some such kind of fashion: again, if our circular travels seem tedious, if our activity seems to have gone astray, perhaps this is just as it should be.